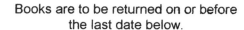
Books are to be returned on or before
the last date below.

KT-558-103

LIBREX-

Leaders

Jilly Hunt

www.raintreepublishers.co.uk
Visit our website to find out
more information about
Raintree books.

To order:
☎ Phone 0845 6044371
🖹 Fax +44 (0) 1865 312263
💻 Email myorders@raintreepublishers.co.uk

Customers from outside the UK please telephone +44 1865 312262

Raintree is an imprint of Capstone Global Library
Limited, a company incorporated in England and Wales
having its registered office at 7 Pilgrim Street, London,
EC4V 6LB – Registered company number: 6695582

Edited by Adam Miller, Louise Galpine, and
    Adrian Vigliano
Designed by Marcus Bell
Original illustrations © Capstone Global Library Ltd
Illustrated by Darren Lingard
Picture research by Tracy Cummins
Production by Alison Parsons
Originated by Capstone Global Library Ltd
Printed and bound in China by Leo Paper Products Ltd.

ISBN 978 1 406 24011 5 (hardback)
16 15 14 13 12
10 9 8 7 6 5 4 3 2 1

British Library Cataloguing in Publication Data
Hunt, Jilly.
Leaders. -- (Ethics of politics)
172.7-dc23
A full catalogue record for this book is available from
the British Library.

Acknowledgements
We would like to thank the following for permission
to reproduce photographs: Corbis pp. 6 (© Pete Souza/
White House/Handout/The White House), 9 (©
Keystone), 11 (© Bettmann), 13, 17, 20 (© Corbis), 29
(© Bettmann), 30 (© Gideon Mendel), 33 (© Reuters),
36 (© Flip Schulke), 43 (© David Furst/Pool/epa), 45
(© Reuters), 46 (© Kapoor Baldev/Sygma), 47 (© Alain
Keler/Sygma), 50 (© Hulton-Deutsch Collection);
Getty Images pp. 7 (National Archive/Newsmakers),
23 (Hulton Archive), 25 (David Hume Kennerly),
27 (Dinodia Photos), 34 (Francis Miller/Time Life
Pictures), 38 (Spencer Platt), 40 (Chris Hondros), 48
(John Moore), 49 (Dirck Halstead), 53 (Keystone/
Hulton Archive); Library of Congress Prints and
Photographs Division pp. 14, 19, 51; Shutterstock pp. 4
(© homeros), 5 (© Sam Dcruz).

Cover photograph of US President Obama reproduced
with the permission of Getty Images (Scott J. Ferrell).

We would like to thank Jonathan Lipman for his
invaluable help in the preparation of this book.

Every effort has been made to contact copyright holders
of any material reproduced in this book. Any omissions
will be rectified in subsequent printings if notice is
given to the publisher.

CONTENTS

Some words are printed in bold, **like this**. You can find out what they mean by looking in the glossary.

POLITICS AND ETHICS

Politics is the way a country, state, or community is run, as well as the way it builds relationships with other governments or communities. The term "politics" comes from the Greek word *polis*, which means "city" or "state".[1]

Leaders are always a part of politics. Different leaders have their own personal styles of leadership, but the way they lead their people usually fits within a certain **political system**. A political system is the general behaviour of a government and the legal institutions it uses. Examples of political systems include **democracy**, **monarchy**, **dictatorship**, and **communism**.

Each type of political system operates in a different way and is based on a different set of beliefs. For example, democracy is government decided by the people. In a democracy, the candidates with the most votes usually win the election. In some democracies, the party with the most winning candidates forms the ruling government. In a monarchy, the rule of a country is passed down through a family, with leaders such as kings and queens. In a dictatorship, just one person rules the government. Some political systems are defined by their **economic** practices. For example, in the system of communism, the state controls every aspect of the **economy**.

In a democracy, people vote for the political party they most want to win.

What are ethics?

Ethics are concerned with what is good or bad, right or wrong. The term "ethics" is also used to describe a person's or government's moral values or principles. Ethics are about how people live their lives.

This book will look at the decisions major leaders of the world have made during key events in history, and how **ethical** these decisions have been. For example, is it justifiable to go to war if it is likely that innocent people will be killed? Is it acceptable to be dishonest if it is for a good cause? Can leaders justify living in luxury while their people are starving? Should leaders be judged on how ethically they have behaved in their personal lives as well as by their **political** careers? This book will explore some of these issues and examine how leaders have responded.

Ideas about ethics can become complicated, with people believing different things. So, who is the judge? If not everyone agrees on the same moral principles, who decides whether a person or government has behaved ethically? Throughout this book, "What do you think?" boxes will help you decide about these issues. These boxes will ask questions that will help you analyse the situation and make up your own mind about what is or is not ethical.

Leaders of a country have to make some difficult decisions, such as whether to go to war, knowing that hundreds or thousands of people may lose their homes or be killed. These people are fleeing from war in the Democratic Republic of Congo.

What is leadership?

Leadership can take many forms. You may be most familiar with leaders in your school or through activities you participate in, such as the head of your school or a sports coach. You may be a leader of a group yourself. This book is about political leaders in control of communities, states, or countries.

Leaders may come into power in different ways, depending on the political system that runs a country. For example, in a democracy a leader will usually be voted in by the people of the country. However, in a dictatorship, the leader may have seized power using military force. In a non-governmental group, the leader may have been elected in a less formal way, perhaps because he or she is thought to have a special talent.

UK prime minister David Cameron and US president Barack Obama were both voted into power under democratic systems.

How does it affect me?

Do you know who leads your country? Investigate what decisions they make on your behalf.

Leading personality

Successful leaders often have similar personality traits.

An ability to communicate is an essential part of successful leadership. US president John F. Kennedy was quiet and shy as a child, yet he is now considered one of the most popular presidents of modern times. He used the **media** to great effect to communicate with the voters of the United States. He had style and charisma, and together with his wife, Jacqueline, he promoted US culture around the world.[2] US president Franklin D. Roosevelt showed his great ability to communicate, as he told the people of America in a fireside chat about the need for backing Britain in World War II even though this might take the country into war.

The style and charisma of the Kennedys won people over.

The power of personality is not always a good thing, however. German leader Adolf Hitler is thought of today as evil in a human form, but he had a strong ability to persuade people. Hitler created a **cult of personality** around himself, meaning he created a sense of devotion among the people who followed him. Posters and other forms of communication promoted Hitler and made him a symbol of strength and virtue. People would greet each other by saying "Heil Hitler" and performing a Nazi salute.[3]

For the good of others

Leadership can also be about working for the good of others. The US **civil rights** leader Martin Luther King Jr became a leader of the African-American community because of his position as a church leader, but also because of his values. He encouraged his followers to take the moral high ground and not to sink to the level of violence that their opponents demonstrated.[4]

Nelson Mandela, the first black president of South Africa, is admired because of his ability to forgive those who imprisoned him for so many years. Instead of seeking revenge on the group that oppressed him, Mandela worked to achieve peace in the country that he loves.[5]

LEADERS DURING WAR: WORLD WAR II

World War II started in Europe in 1939, and by its end in 1945 it had involved nearly every part of the world. On one side were the Allied powers, made up of the United Kingdom, France, Poland, Australia, and eventually the United States and the **Soviet Union**, among others. On the other side were the Axis powers, made up of Germany, Italy, Japan, and others.

The war started when Adolf Hitler's German army invaded Poland on 1 September 1939. Over the course of the war, UK prime minister Winston Churchill, US president Franklin D. Roosevelt, and Soviet leader Joseph Stalin all played important leadership roles.[1] War presents leaders with many ethical decisions to make. Read on and judge for yourself about the decisions these leaders made.

Hitler enters politics

On 12 September 1919, Hitler entered politics when he gave a speech about the evils of communism.[2] The world did not know it, but this was the start of one of the most brutal chapters of history.

By July 1921, Hitler was in charge of the National Socialist German Workers' Party (*Nationalsozialistische Deutsche Arbeiterpartei*).[3] This was shortened to the Nazi Party. Hitler was a very persuasive public speaker, and under his leadership membership of the Nazi Party grew. The Nazi Party wanted to see a larger Germany that united all German-speaking people in Europe. Their demands included extra living space for German people, banning Jews from being considered German citizens, gaining adequate pensions for elderly people, and sharing the profits from big industries.[4]

What do you think?

Do the demands of the Nazi Party seem reasonable? How would Germany get more living space? Whom would they take it from? Is it ever acceptable to take away the rights of a race or a religion? Can you think of other occasions when this has happened?

Führer of Germany

On 30 January 1933, German president Paul von Hindenburg made Hitler **chancellor**. But Hitler was not satisfied with just being chancellor. He wanted more power. He did not have to wait long. President Hindenburg died at the age of 87 on 2 August 1934.[5] Hitler announced that the positions of chancellor and president were now joined together, and that he would be the *führer* (leader) of Germany. He had total control and set about turning Germany into a Nazi state under his rule as **dictator**.

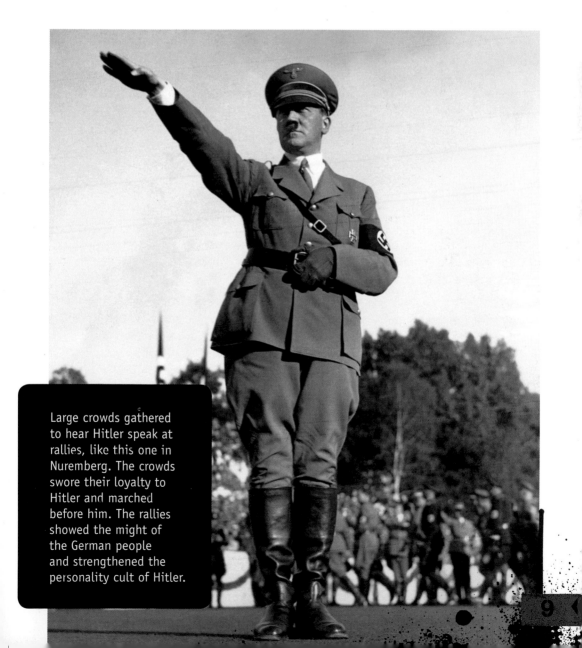

Large crowds gathered to hear Hitler speak at rallies, like this one in Nuremberg. The crowds swore their loyalty to Hitler and marched before him. The rallies showed the might of the German people and strengthened the personality cult of Hitler.

Nazi terror tactics

Hitler used his personal bodyguards (called the *Schutzstaffel*, or SS) and his secret police (called the Gestapo) to terrify people into obeying him. Many people who did not agree with the Nazi party were imprisoned in **concentration camps**.

The Nazis "educated" people into their way of thinking by rewriting textbooks. Teachers who refused to teach Nazi ideas were imprisoned. From 1936, boys aged 13 and over were made to join a group called the Hitler Youth. In this group, boys would be given military training and taught to hate Jews. Girls would be taught that women should stay at home and raise Aryan children, meaning children with no Jewish blood. Children were encouraged to report adults they encountered whose views did not agree with the Nazi ideals.[6]

What do you think?

Was Hitler educating the German people or brainwashing them? Is it ethical to "educate" or train people into thinking a certain way?

Persecution

Hitler wanted to create a "pure" race of Germans. He hated groups such as Jews, gypsies, homosexuals, and disabled people. He **persecuted** these groups. For example, in 1935, he introduced what were called the Nuremberg Laws. These laws stated that German Jews were no longer citizens of Germany.[7] In 1938, when a Jew murdered a German politician, the Nazis used this as an excuse to attack Jews in Germany. The Nazis burned down 267 synagogues, smashed the windows of 8,000 Jewish stores, and murdered 91 Jewish people. They arrested thousands of Jews and sent them to concentration camps. Six million Jews died in these camps, and this has become known as the **Holocaust**.[8]

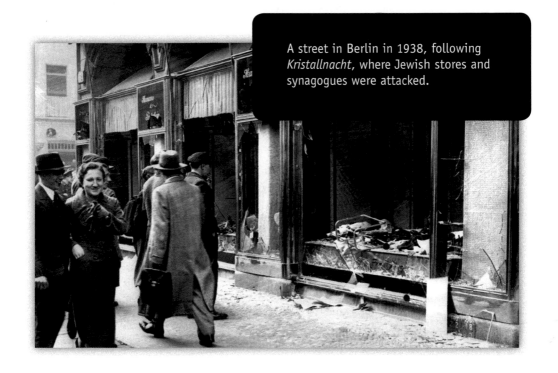

A street in Berlin in 1938, following *Kristallnacht*, where Jewish stores and synagogues were attacked.

Churchill's warnings

In the 1930s, politician Winston Churchill delivered many warnings about the threat of Hitler and the Nazis. He was shocked by Hitler's treatment of the Jews. He argued that the United Kingdom should take the threat of Hitler's Germany seriously.

Churchill collected information about the amount of weapons the Germans had acquired since World War I (1914–1918).[9] Germany had lost that war and, as part of an agreement that ended the war, it was not supposed to be building up its weapons supplies. Churchill was worried that the German air force, called the *Luftwaffe*, would become as powerful as the Royal Air Force. But Churchill was often ignored. Many UK leaders at the time did not want to act.[10]

The prime minister in 1938, Neville Chamberlain, thought that Germany could be allowed to take over an area of Czechoslovakia. Germany, France, and Italy agreed. Chamberlain thought that this compromise would stop Germany from invading anywhere else. He told the British people that he had achieved "peace with honour" and that he believed it was "peace in our time" – in other words, that he had prevented a war. Churchill disagreed. He said, "You were given the choice between war and dishonour. You chose dishonour and you will have war."

Declaration of war

When the United Kingdom declared war on Germany in September 1939, Churchill was recalled to the cabinet, the group of senior ministers responsible for setting government policy in the United Kingdom. They were ready to listen to him now. By May 1940, Churchill was prime minister.

Within two weeks of Churchill taking office, Belgium had surrendered to Germany, France was losing battles and looked like it would be captured, and the United Kingdom was struggling to defend itself.[11]

Forming alliances

Churchill knew he had to form **alliances** with other countries to help fight Germany. He called upon the "New World, with all its power and might" (meaning the United States) to rescue the Old World (meaning Europe).[12]

The United States had been supplying the United Kingdom and France with weapons. In 1940, when it seemed like the United Kingdom was all alone in its fight, US president Roosevelt convinced **Congress** to support the United Kingdom with "all aid short of war".[13] The United States then officially entered World War II in December 1941, following the Japanese attack on Pearl Harbor in Hawaii, where US soldiers were stationed.[14]

A less likely **ally** for the United Kingdom, however, was the Soviet Union. This was a huge **communist** state (made up of many republics) led by Russia and its dictator Joseph Stalin. Churchill thought that communism was a threat to peace, but at the same time the Soviet Union was also being attacked by Hitler. Churchill stated in a broadcast on 22 June 1941: "The Russian danger … is our danger" and promised to help the Soviet people.[15]

The agreement among the United Kingdom, the United States, and the Soviet Union became known as the Grand Alliance. It was Churchill who held these crucial relationships together. He travelled from one country to another to meet personally with Roosevelt and Stalin to keep the alliance together.[16]

What do you think?

If you were Churchill, would you have joined forces with the Soviet Union – a country you did not trust and which could be a future enemy – in order to fight a current enemy such as Hitler?

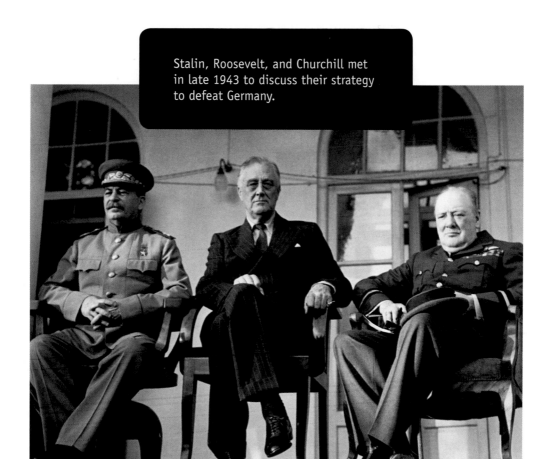

Stalin, Roosevelt, and Churchill met in late 1943 to discuss their strategy to defeat Germany.

WINSTON CHURCHILL

Born: 30 November 1874, Blenheim Palace, Oxfordshire

Died: 24 January 1965, London

Winston Churchill was born into a life of privilege to New York society beauty Jennie Jerome and her husband, Lord Randolph Churchill, who held a powerful position in the UK government. At the age of 16, Churchill entered the military college, Sandhurst, where he excelled in studies of tactics and fortifications. This knowledge was important for the role he was to play in later life as prime minister during World War II. Churchill gained experience with war as a soldier, observer, and journalist in conflicts throughout the world. After World War II, in 1953, Churchill was knighted by Queen Elizabeth II. In 1963, he was made an honorary citizen of the United States.[17]

Stalin's position

Stalin had come to power in 1929 and ruled as a ruthless dictator (see box below).[18] He had played an important role in Hitler's rise to power. Stalin was in control of the International Communist Party and would not allow the German Communist Party to go against Hitler. He thought that a Nazi victory in Germany would be a victory for the communists, because **capitalism** would be defeated.[19]

JOSEPH STALIN

Born: 18 December 1879, Gori, Georgia, Russian Empire

Died: 5 March 1953, Moscow, Russia, Soviet Union

Joseph Stalin was secretary-general of the Communist Party of the Soviet Union from 1922 to 1953 and premier of the Soviet Union from 1941 until his death in 1953. His ruthless dictatorship helped make the Soviet Union into a major world power.

Stalin ensured that he had no political enemies by using his secret police force to remove them. He caused the death by starvation of millions of farmers who disagreed with his plans to transform the countryside into state-organized farms. This was during a period known as the Great Terror. Millions of people were killed by starvation – estimates range from 3 million to more than 10 million people.

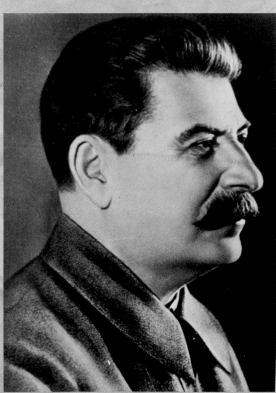

By mid-1934, it was clear that Stalin was wrong – a Nazi victory was not a communist victory. Germany was expanding into Austria and Czechoslovakia. In 1938, the Soviet Union, the United Kingdom, and France were trying to reach an alliance against Germany, but had not yet been successful. Germany was getting closer to Soviet territory. In early 1939, as the Soviet Union seemed alone in resisting German expansion into Eastern Europe, Stalin tried a change of tactic.[20]

What do you think?

Was Stalin doing the right thing by agreeing to a pact with Germany? After all, it seemed to protect the Soviet people from being attacked by the Germans. Or do you think Stalin was thinking about the increase in power that it would allow him?

In August 1939, Stalin and Hitler made a pact that they would not attack each other.[21] Stalin wanted to increase Soviet territory, and this pact would allow him time to build up his army. A secret part of the pact was that all of Eastern Europe would be divided up between Germany and the Soviet Union. Hitler could invade Poland, France, and the United Kingdom without the risk of being attacked by the Soviet Union. Yet on 22 June 1941, Germany attacked the Soviet Union.[22]

Europe first

At the end of 1940, US president Roosevelt and his advisers were making strategic plans about what would happen if the United States became involved in the war. They decided that they would put "Europe first" and just have defensive operations in the Pacific. The UK and the United States made plans about how to support the Soviet Union. However, Japan's entry into the war and bombing of Pearl Harbor on 7 December 1941, changed these plans. The Soviets did not get the support they were hoping for.

Churchill, Roosevelt, and their advisers held a big meeting on 22 December 1941. This ended with the signing of the Declaration of the **United Nations** on 1 January 1942. The declaration was a statement of common aims for both the United Kingdom and the United States.

With strengthened forces to fight him, Hitler realized that he had no hope of winning the war. To avoid capture, he committed suicide on 30 April 1945. Germany surrendered on 8 May 1945. The war in the Pacific ended when Japan officially surrendered on 2 September 1945. World War II marked a shift in power away from Western Europe towards the United States and the Soviet Union.

THE COLD WAR (1945–1991)

Following the defeat of Germany in World War II, the alliance among the United Kingdom, the United States, and the Soviet Union seemed set to split.

The Soviet Union had made great advances into Eastern Europe. Stalin wanted control of a large part of Central and Eastern Europe. In the countries he had occupied or "liberated", he had initially agreed to restore the previous government or hold elections. But Stalin began to put governments in places that he controlled.

At the same time, the UK and US governments feared the spread of communism. In 1946, Churchill said, "An iron curtain has descended across the Continent [of Europe]."[1] Europe was split into communist and non-communist countries. The **Cold War** had begun.

The Cold War was not a war that was fought directly on the battlefields by the United States and the Soviet Union. Instead it was a period of extreme tension and competition between these two **superpowers**. The United States feared the spread of communism, while the Soviet Union wanted to maintain control of Eastern European countries, to protect its borders from another German attack. At the same time, it wanted to spread the Ideals of communism around the world.

What added to the tension was that both countries now possessed **nuclear weapons**. War would not be the same again. A nuclear attack could cause devastation.

John F. Kennedy enters politics

At the start of the Cold War, John F. Kennedy entered politics. The Cold War would dominate his political life. In January 1961, Kennedy was sworn in as president of the United States. The departing president, Dwight D. Eisenhower, gave Kennedy a briefing about his new job. The first thing he told him about was the black satchel that went everywhere with the president, carried by two military officers. The satchel contained the codes needed to start or respond to a nuclear war.[2]

On 6 December 1960, President-elect John F. Kennedy is welcomed into the White House by President Dwight Eisenhower.

The next part of the briefing was about the trouble spots around the world where the Cold War was being fought. Instead of directly fighting each other, which would have involved the use of nuclear weapons, the two superpowers supported opposing sides in disputes around the world. In Southeast Asia, the United States was helping Laos and South Vietnam fight civil wars against communists backed by the Soviet Union. In Germany, the city of Berlin was divided. The east side was communist and the west side was **democratic**. US and Soviet troops had occupied the divided city since the end of World War II.

What do you think?

How do you think the ownership of nuclear weapons changed the way countries did battle? Is it ethical to support the wars of other countries in order to fight a bigger war?

Which battle to fight?

Kennedy needed to decide where to put his resources. The communists in Laos seemed to be winning that war, and Laos was a difficult country to defend. But Vietnam had a long coastline where the US Navy could bring in supplies. Plus, Vietnam's president was anti-communist. Kennedy negotiated a peace deal with the Soviet Union over Laos, which included a **neutral** government. However, Kennedy knew this government would not be strong enough to hold power, and that the communists would soon take over.

What do you think?

Was it ethical for Kennedy to pull out US support for Laos and agree to a deal that he knew would not last? Kennedy knew that most Americans did not know where Laos was, so they would not be too concerned about whether or not the United States pulled out. Should that have influenced his decision?

Cuba and Fidel Castro

Cuba was a country that worried more Americans. It is only 140 kilometres (87 miles) from the United States, and so what happened there might have more of an impact.[3] The communist leader of Cuba was Fidel Castro. He had come to power in January 1959, after overthrowing the former **corrupt** government.

Castro declared that a dictator would never run Cuba again, but in fact he became a communist dictator himself. He had his enemies executed and he imprisoned those who were disloyal to him. In 1959 and 1960, he took control of the property of big US businesses based in Cuba. The United States responded by refusing to buy Cuban sugar. So, Castro turned to the Soviet Union for trade and support. The United States cut off **diplomatic** relations with Cuba on 3 January 1961.[4]

By the time Kennedy became president, a plan was already in place to overthrow Castro's **regime**. The United States secretly supported anti-Castro Cuban **exiles** in an attack on Cuba's Bay of Pigs, on 17 April 1961. But the attempt failed, because Castro's spies had told him all about it.

As the attack went badly, Kennedy refused to send in the US Air Force to help, because he did not want the United States to be directly connected with it. Kennedy thought that if the Soviets knew the United States was behind it, they would cause trouble in Berlin. Former president Eisenhower thought this was a bad decision. He said, "If they [the Soviets] see us show any weakness that is when they press us the hardest."[5]

Fidel Castro in his military uniform in 1959, arriving in Washington, DC, USA.

Personal relations with Nikita Khrushchev

Kennedy wanted to develop a personal relationship with the head of the Soviet Union, Nikita Khrushchev. The pair met in Vienna, Austria, in June 1961. Kennedy wanted to ensure that a nuclear war would not be started accidentally because of a misunderstanding.

Kennedy and Khrushchev at their meeting in June 1961.

Khrushchev suspected Kennedy was inexperienced and weak. He wanted Kennedy to sign a peace treaty that would recognize East Germany and give the Soviets control over West Berlin. The German city of Berlin had been divided since World War II, with the Soviets controlling East Berlin and the West controlling West Berlin. Khrushchev was concerned about the number of East Germans fleeing to the West via Berlin and the effect that this was having on the East German economy.

Khrushchev tried to threaten Kennedy. He said, "I want peace. But if you want war, that is your problem." Kennedy stood up to the bullying tactics of Khrushchev. He announced in a speech on 3 August 1961, that the United States would increase its military spending. Kennedy was showing that he was prepared to go to war. He declared that an attack on West Berlin was "an attack upon us all".

Shortly after, on 12 August 1961, the Berlin Wall was built by the East German government as a barrier between East and West Germany. This was a sign that Khrushchev had backed down. Kennedy said about the wall: "It's not a very nice solution, but a wall is a hell of a lot better than a war."[6]

What do you think?

Was it ethical for Khrushchev to threaten war to get his way? Should Khrushchev have built the wall? Was he imprisoning the East German people?

Cuba not forgotten

In late 1961, the United States made a plan called "Operation Mongoose", which aimed to remove Castro as leader of Cuba. This was the start of an undeclared war. The **Central Intelligence Agency (CIA)** trained Cuban agents. In Cuba, they blew up factories and bridges, set fire to crops, and killed Cuban officials.

Castro was convinced that this was the start of a US invasion, and so he turned to Khrushchev for support. Khrushchev used the opportunity to secretly install nuclear weapons in Cuba in April 1962. While the missiles could be seen as defending Cuba, it also meant the Soviet Union had control of nuclear missiles that could easily reach the United States. This was much cheaper for the Soviet Union than developing new long-range missiles that had to be fired from the Soviet Union. Khrushchev also disliked the fact that the United States had missile bases close to the Soviet Union, in Turkey. Now they were even.[7]

Life in Castro's Cuba

Fidel Castro took control of all aspects of the lives of the Cuban people. He had control over politics, economics, and cultural life. Anyone who opposed him politically was ruthlessly suppressed. Yet Castro expanded Cuba's social services, such as health and education, and made them available to everyone without charge. He also guaranteed employment for everyone. Castro was not a good economic manager, though, and Cuba's economy failed to grow. It depended heavily on the export of sugarcane and on its favourable trade policies with the Soviets, which came to an end in 1991.[8]

The Cuban Missile Crisis

In October 1962, the United States discovered that Soviet missile bases were being built in Cuba. US spy planes had taken photographs of them. Kennedy was furious. He declared that any attack by Cuba would be seen as an attack by the Soviets. The two superpowers were on the brink of a nuclear war.[9]

JOHN F. KENNEDY

Born: 29 May 1917, Brookline, Massachusetts, USA

Died: 22 November 1963, Dallas, Texas, USA

John F. Kennedy was pressured into politics by his father, Joseph Kennedy. In 1957, he began his campaign to become president of the United States. Backed by his father's money, Kennedy had an expensive publicity campaign that helped increase his popularity. However, Kennedy had two major disadvantages working against him. First, he was Catholic, while the United States was a largely Protestant country and had never had a Catholic president. Second, he was young and had no experience in a senior role in government.

Nevertheless, Kennedy won the 1960 general election. He defeated the Republican candidate, Richard Nixon, by fewer than 120,000 votes out of a total of over 70,000,000 votes.[10] Kennedy was a popular president, but on 22 November 1963, he was **assassinated** while taking part in a parade in Dallas.

Kennedy had to decide what to do. The United States did not want to negotiate with the Soviets. They discussed attacking the Cuban missile bases, but they were worried that the Soviet Union would attack West Berlin in retaliation. And once the actual fighting had started, where would it stop? The United States instead imposed a quarantine on ships. This was a block by the US Navy on any Soviet ships bringing weapons into Cuba.

What do you think?

Should the United States have carried out "Operation Mongoose"? Were the Soviets justified in placing missiles in Cuba? Was the welfare of Cuban citizens ever considered during the Cuban Missile Crisis?

Khrushchev's response

Khrushchev's plan had backfired. Instead of strengthening his position, he had brought on the threat of attack. Khrushchev knew he could not win this war, because the Soviet Union did not have as much money as the United States to spend on weapons and the military. He had to find a way to prevent war but maintain his pride.

Castro and Khrushchev met in the Soviet capital, Moscow, in 1964.

Kennedy and Khrushchev wrote to each other. Khrushchev promised not to send weapons to Cuba if Kennedy promised not to attack and also to remove the US weapons from Turkey. Kennedy replied that he would not attack if Khrushchev removed the weapons from Cuba. There was no mention of the missiles in Turkey (although this was discussed in secret diplomatic meetings).

Meanwhile, Castro was not going to wait to be told what to do to defend his country. He ordered his troops to fire on US planes. Khrushchev realized that he was losing control of Castro, and so he agreed to remove the missiles from. Cuba. The crisis was over. Castro was furious at Khrushchev's withdrawal, but there was nothing he could do about it.

The Cold War continues

The Cold War continued into the 1970s and 1980s. The early 1980s saw an increase in tension, as the two superpowers continued to build up their weapon collections and compete for influence in countries in Africa and Central America.

In 1981, former film star and governor of California, Ronald Reagan, became president of the United States. At the same time, the United Kingdom was ruled by its first woman prime minister, Margaret Thatcher. Reagan and Thatcher continued the positive relationship between the United States and the United Kingdom. Both leaders were against communism. Reagan's comments about the Soviet Union led to a worsening of relations with the Soviet Union. He called the Soviet Union "an evil empire" and "the focus of evil in the modern world".[11] Thatcher earned the nickname "Iron Lady" from the Soviet media because of her strong anti-communist beliefs.[12]

In 1983, Reagan announced on television a proposal for a space-based missile defence system. This was given the nickname "Star Wars", after the popular science-fiction film. The system was intended to defend the United States against Soviet attack. However, in truth – and unknown to the Soviets – the United States did not yet have the technology to make the system work as described.[13]

An unlikely partnership

In March 1985, Mikhail Gorbachev became leader of the Soviet Union. He seemed to be someone with whom the United States and the United Kingdom could work.

At this time, the Soviet Union was experiencing a long-term decline in its economy. The people were also experiencing a lower life expectancy (average number of years lived) and higher infant mortality rate (number of babies not surviving). Gorbachev introduced a series of policy reforms called perestroika (meaning "reconstruction") and glasnost (meaning "openness"). This would make the Soviet Union become more liberal. By 1988, the country was moving towards democracy. The policy of glasnost turned into freedom of speech, something the Soviet Union had not experienced for decades.

Gorbachev's foreign policy was called the "new political thinking". It was based on the idea that all countries had the right to decide their political and economic systems. Countries in East and Central Europe embraced this ideal and left the Soviet Union and communism. Gorbachev did not expect this to happen, but he did not use any military force to stop it, as previous Soviet leaders would have done.[14]

The Soviet Union eventually collapsed in 1991. The Cold War came to an end.

What do you think?

Gorbachev's critics thought that he had lost the power and territory that the Soviet Union had gained during the fighting in World War II, which had cost the lives of 27 million Soviet citizens.[15] What do you think? Should Gorbachev have tried to prevent the collapse of the Soviet Union?

US president Ronald Reagan and Soviet leader Mikhail Gorbachev pose for the cameras at their second summit meeting in 1986.

THE FIGHT FOR CIVIL RIGHTS (1915–1994)

Throughout the 20th century, people in places ranging from India to South Africa to the United States made huge strides in the fight for equality and freedom. The fight for these rights continues in many places around the world today.

India: Gandhi and Nehru

In India, Mohandas Gandhi was a great leader in the fight for civil rights. In 1888, when he was 19 years old, Gandhi left India to study law in London. Racism was common in the United Kingdom at this time, and so Gandhi's fellow students snubbed him. He spent his time reading, and he studied philosophy.

In US writer Henry David Thoreau's book *Civil Disobedience*, Gandhi discovered the principle of non-violence – or **civil disobedience**. He was also influenced by British writer John Ruskin, who wanted a move out of the cities and away from industrialization in favour of a return to the countryside and agriculture. The theories of these two writers fit in with Gandhi's religious and cultural beliefs. They shaped his later campaigns for social justice, civil rights, and **agrarian** values.[1]

Between 1893 and 1914, Gandhi worked as a lawyer in South Africa.[2] Here Gandhi experienced even more racism. A white driver beat Gandhi up because he would not make room for a European passenger. What he witnessed in South Africa provoked him into action. He began to bring people's attention to injustices. He also gained the attention of newspapers in London and India.

When the South African (Boer) War started in 1899, in reaction to the United Kingdom's presence there, Gandhi persuaded his fellow Indians in South Africa to join the UK side. He argued that if Indians wanted full rights as UK citizens, they should also be prepared to contribute to the war effort. He formed an ambulance division of 1,100 Indian volunteers.[3]

Mohandas Gandhi became a symbol of peaceful resistance in the struggle for an independent India.

What do you think?

Was Gandhi right to ask Indians in South Africa to contribute to the war effort? Notice that Gandhi was not asking them to do any fighting, but rather just to help care for wounded or dying soldiers.

Devotion to truth

It was in South Africa that Gandhi introduced the concept of *satyagraha*, meaning "devotion to or insistence on truth" in the Hindi language. This was a non-violent resistance to evil, and it became a major part of Gandhi's later fight against UK rule in India.

Protest groups in other countries have since adopted the technique. It involves inviting suffering on oneself, rather than inflicting it on others. Hundreds of Indians sacrificed themselves by suffering imprisonment, floggings (whippings), and even shootings in order to protest against their treatment. The technique worked. The South African government did not look good and experienced pressure from the United Kingdom and India to change things.

By 1920, Gandhi was back in India and becoming an influential person in Indian politics – and in the fight for Indian independence from the United Kingdom, which ruled India at the time. Gandhi and the Indian National Congress Party led a programme of "non-violent non-cooperation" with the UK government in India. Gandhi led three major campaigns – from 1920 to 1922, 1930 to 1934, and 1940 to 1942.[4] Between these times he was not actively involved in Indian politics, and for some of this time he was in prison for his resistance activities. By 1942, Gandhi's partner in fighting for an independent India was recognized as Jawaharlal Nehru.[5]

Jawaharlal Nehru

When Nehru became the vice president of India's government in 1946, he faced a dilemma. The relationship between Hindus and Muslims in India was tense, and riots broke out between 1946 and 1947.[6] Nehru was in discussions with the UK government and a group called the Muslim League.[7] The Muslim League wanted India to be divided based on religion. After World War II, the United Kingdom was in debt and saw India as a financial burden. Dividing India along religious lines seemed the fastest way to settle the problem and relieve itself of the burden.

Nehru and Gandhi were not happy with the solution of dividing India, yet there seemed no alternative. Nehru reluctantly agreed. India was to be divided, and a new country, Pakistan, was created for India's Muslim population. However, peace was not achieved. The state of Kashmir was disputed, as both sides wanted ownership. India sent in troops to defend Kashmir, and a United Nations (UN) ceasefire was eventually negotiated. However, the region is still unstable today.

Gandhi on the steps of his home, accompanied by colleagues including Jawaharlal Nehru.

Nehru ruled as India's prime minister until his death in 1964. Nehru agreed with Gandhi's principles. However, unlike Gandhi, he did not want India to follow an agrarian system. Instead, Nehru wanted modernization in India. He brought modern ways of thinking into India and adapted them to suit India's needs. He wanted India to be up to date in terms of scientific discoveries and technological development.

Nehru was ruler of India at the time of the Cold War. He had to decide whether India was going to take sides with the United States or the Soviet Union. Instead, he introduced a policy of **non-alignment**. This meant India did not take either side and tried to remain neutral in international affairs.[8]

South Africa: Mandela and de Klerk

South Africa introduced **apartheid** in 1950 (see box below right). As a result, the black majority was discriminated against even more than before by the Afrikaner white minority who ruled the country.

South African police charged this group of peaceful protestors who were marching to a prison in Cape Town, South Africa, to demand the release of political prisoners.

In 1944, a young black African lawyer called Nelson Mandela joined the African National Congress (ANC). The ANC was a political group trying to achieve voting rights for blacks and people of mixed race in South Africa. Mandela held various leadership positions in the ANC and helped oppose the apartheid policies.[9]

Peaceful protests

Following the example and success of Gandhi's non-violent civil disobedience, the ANC adopted the same strategy in the early 1950s. The ANC leaders agreed that, like Gandhi, they must be prepared to be imprisoned for their beliefs.[10] Yet India was dealing with a foreign power (the United Kingdom) that, according to Mandela, "was more realistic and far-sighted" than the Afrikaners in South Africa.[11]

Mandela would follow Gandhi's strategy of non-violent disobedience for as long as it worked. However, unlike Gandhi, Mandela did not follow this strategy because of moral principle. When peaceful protests were met with violence, Mandela felt that the strategy needed to change. In 1953, Mandela made a speech to this effect, but the leaders of the ANC did not approve. The use of violence was not the group's policy, and it was worried that using violence would give the authorities an excuse to use even more violence to harm the ANC and its supporters.[12]

What do you think?

Was Mandela right to suggest the use of violence when it seemed peaceful protests were not working?

Apartheid

Apartheid is an Afrikaans word that means "apartness". In 1948, the white South African government introduced a policy that meant that South Africans were divided up into racial groups: white, "native" (black), and "coloured" (those of mixed race). They later added a fourth group, "Asian", which consisted mainly of Indians. A system of **segregation** kept these groups apart.

Blacks, people of mixed race, and Asians were discriminated against in all areas of life, from what jobs they could do to where they could live to which schools they could attend. They had no influence in government. The white government introduced laws that allowed the police to arrest anyone it suspected of opposing government policies. The police were legally allowed to torture and kill. Arrested people were kept without trial and denied access to lawyers and their families.[13]

State of emergency

In 1960, in the black township of Sharpeville, South Africa, the police fired on a crowd of unarmed blacks, killing or wounding about 250 people. In response, 20,000 blacks demonstrated near the police station at Sharpeville and started throwing stones at the police. The police shot at them with submachine guns. About 11,000 people were arrested, and a state of emergency was declared.

The ANC and a breakaway group, the Pan-Africanist Congress (PAC), were banned in South Africa. In 1961, Mandela went "underground" and was one of the founding members of the Spear of the Nation group. He trained for guerrilla warfare (irregular fighting) and sabotage (destroying property and creating confusion). He was arrested and sentenced to five years in prison. While in prison, Mandela was convicted of sabotage, treason (acting against his country), and violent conspiracy. He was sentenced to life imprisonment.[14]

In his defence, Mandela made a speech that has since become famous. He explained what black Africans were fighting for: "Africans just wanted a share in the whole of South Africa." He acknowledged that white voters would fear the blacks getting the vote because they thought it would lead to black domination. He said, "The ANC had spent half a century fighting against racialism. When it triumphs it will not change that policy." Mandela spoke of the "ideal of a democratic and free society in which all persons live together in harmony and with equal opportunities". He said, "It is an ideal which I hope to live for and to achieve. But if need be, it is an ideal for which I am prepared to die."[15]

Imprisonment

Throughout Mandela's imprisonment, he and other members of the ANC continued to protest against the policies of the government. One accepted method of protest was the hunger strike. Gandhi had used this as a form of protest, too. But Mandela felt that it was punishing the prisoners, not the authorities. Instead he wanted to punish the authorities. The authorities wanted to see a clean and tidy prison yard, so prisoners left it untidy. These techniques distressed and exasperated the authorities.[16]

F. W. de Klerk and the end of apartheid

The Sharpeville massacre drew international attention to the discrimination in South Africa, and many countries imposed economic **sanctions**. People all over the world campaigned for an end to apartheid.

In the late 1980s – nearly 30 years after Sharpeville – the South African government held secret discussions with Mandela. In 1989, F. W. de Klerk became president and sped up the end of apartheid. In 1990, he freed Mandela and other political prisoners. Mandela had been a prisoner for 27 years. The ban was lifted on the ANC and the PAC. By 1992, a peaceful transition to democracy was underway.

In April 1994, South Africa had its first election in which all races could vote. Mandela's ANC party won, and Mandela became South Africa's first black president. De Klerk was his deputy president.[17]

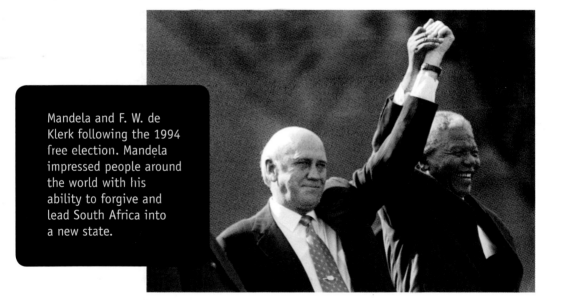

Mandela and F. W. de Klerk following the 1994 free election. Mandela impressed people around the world with his ability to forgive and lead South Africa into a new state.

President Mandela

In his position as president of South Africa, Mandela introduced initiatives to improve housing, education, and the living standards of South Africa's blacks. He created the Truth and Reconciliation Commission, which investigated human rights violations under apartheid.[18] But he did not seek revenge for his treatment by whites. Instead, Mandela said: "If there are dreams about a beautiful South Africa, there are also roads that lead to their goal. Two of these roads could be named Goodness and Forgiveness."[19]

The United States: Martin Luther King Jr and John F. Kennedy

In the United States in the 1950s and 1960s, the fight for civil rights for African Americans heated up. Unlike India and South Africa, African Americans were supposed to have had equal rights under the law ever since the end of slavery in 1865. However, in the southern states in particular, racial discrimination continued.[20]

Rosa Parks

On 1 December 1955, an African-American woman called Rosa Parks refused to give up her bus seat to a white passenger in Montgomery, Alabama. Parks was breaking the segregation laws in Montgomery that prevented African Americans from sitting on certain seats of a bus if a white person wanted to use them. Parks was arrested, and this triggered a series of events that changed civil rights in the United States.

Martin Luther King Jr during his famous "I have a dream" speech (see page 37).

In particular, this event led to the formation of a group called the Montgomery Improvement Association (MIA). The MIA chose a Baptist minister called Martin Luther King Jr to be its leader. The MIA had success with its bus **boycotts** in Montgomery, when all African Americans in Montgomery refused to use the buses until the segregation policy ended. King realized that to continue with this success, he needed to be able to reach more people. He organized the Southern Christian Leadership Conference (SCLC) and gave lectures and discussed race issues with civil rights and religious leaders across the United States.[21]

Civil disobedience

King was a well-educated man who had studied the great philosophers and religious thinkers as part of his studies in divinity (religion). Like Gandhi, King admired the writer Henry David Thoreau and his book *Civil Disobedience*. King also admired Gandhi, who had put the theory of civil disobedience to the test in his non-violent protests for the rights of Indians and for an independent India.

In February 1959, King got the chance to meet with Indian prime minister Jawaharlal Nehru. They discussed the concept of peaceful non-compliance as used by Nehru and Gandhi in their struggle for Indian independence. King also looked at the fight for equality in South Africa for inspiration. He was convinced that non-violent resistance was the best way forward.[22]

Arrest

In October 1960, King supported local African-American college students in Atlanta, Georgia, who were protesting at a department store that was segregating customers. They chose a **sit-in** as their form of protest. King and 33 others were arrested. The charges for this demonstration were dropped, but King was sentenced to prison for minor traffic offences.

This got the attention of the national media. Georgia was not acting legally by allowing segregation, and the US president, Dwight D. Eisenhower, did nothing to stop it. It was only after the Democratic presidential candidate, John F. Kennedy, intervened that King was released. It is thought that Kennedy's intervention helped him win the Election Day victory that came only eight days later. Many African Americans voted for Kennedy in the hope that he would change things for the better.[23]

More action

King was frustrated by how slowly the government was moving, and he wanted to see more action. So, in 1963, he organized a campaign of sit-ins, boycotts, and mass marches in Birmingham, Alabama. He believed Birmingham to be the most racist city in the South. King was arrested on 12 April 1963, during one of the marches.[24]

By the end of April, the protests were lacking volunteers, so it was suggested that schoolchildren take part. The nation was shocked by the television images showing the violence used by the police. Images showed children being knocked down by high-pressure water hoses and being attacked by police dogs.[25]

The new president, John F. Kennedy, had to act. Kennedy submitted a new Civil Rights Act to Congress. This would outlaw major forms of discrimination like segregation. He made a speech on national television and said: "Are we to say to the world, and much more importantly to each other, that this is the land of the free except for the Negroes [black people], that we have no second class citizens except for the Negroes?" But would Congress pass the bill and make it law?

Martin Luther King Jr and other civil rights leaders meeting President Kennedy and Vice President Lyndon Johnson.

March on Washington

On 28 August 1963, King addressed a crowd of more than 200,000 people who marched on Washington, DC, to demand jobs and freedom for all. He gave a powerful speech that has become known as his "I have a dream" speech.

"I have a dream that one day this nation will rise up and live out the true meaning of its creed: 'We hold these truths to be self-evident that all men are created equal...'"

from Martin Luther King Jr's "I have a dream" speech

What do you think?

Look up Martin Luther King's "I Have a Dream" speech and discover what all his future hopes were.

The March on Washington was a success. But in November 1963, President Kennedy was assassinated. King was greatly saddened by this. He also thought that it was likely he, too, would die young.[26]

The Civil Rights Act was passed in 1964 by the new president, Lyndon B. Johnson.

In April 1968, King made what turned out to be his final speech. He said, "I've seen the promised land. I may not get there with you. But I want you to know tonight, that we, as a people will get to the promised land."[27] The next day he was shot and killed by a white man. Riots broke out in over 100 cities across the United States in reaction to King's death.

THE GLOBAL WAR ON TERROR (2001–2011)

On a sunny morning on 11 September 2001, the world witnessed a truly shocking event. Terrorists boarded and took control of four planes from airports on the east coast of the United States. At 8.46 a.m. (local time), terrorists flew the first plane into the north tower of the World Trade Center in New York City. Seventeen minutes later, a second plane hit the south tower. The buildings were ablaze and badly damaged. At 9.37 a.m., a third plane struck the Pentagon, the headquarters of the US Department of Defense in Washington, DC. A fourth plane crashed in the countryside in Pennsylvania, after its passengers tried to overthrow the terrorists.

The shocking sight of the World Trade Center in flames after two planes were deliberately flown into the twin towers.

About 2,750 people died in the New York attack, 184 died at the Pentagon, and 40 people died in Pennsylvania. All 19 terrorists also died.[1] US president George W. Bush made a speech on 11 September in which he stated: "We will make no distinction between the terrorists who committed these acts and those who harbour them."[2] The global war on terror was about to begin.

The hunt for the terrorists

The hunt was on for those responsible for planning these attacks. The United States soon gathered convincing evidence that an Islamic **militant** group called al-Qaeda, led by Osama bin Laden, was to blame. Bin Laden had made many statements against the United States in the past, and al-Qaeda had been found to take part in other terrorist strikes.

Al-Qaeda was based in Afghanistan and had a close relationship with a militia (military) group called the **Taliban**, which had control of Afghanistan. The United States demanded that bin Laden be handed over to the United States and that the Taliban stop supporting al-Qaeda activity in Afghanistan. The Taliban refused.[3]

UK prime minister Tony Blair had a good relationship with President Bush. He was ready to play a key role in forming a **coalition** to remove the Taliban from power and to fight the global war on terror.

The invasion of Afghanistan

The first step was to remove the Taliban from Afghanistan and dismantle al-Qaeda. The CIA worked covertly with anti-Taliban groups in Afghanistan to come up with a strategy to overthrow the Taliban. Bush hoped that by working with the Afghans, he would not have to send many US troops to fight. The CIA team and Afghans were joined by US and UK special forces. On 7 October 2001, US and UK war planes targeted Taliban strongholds. The Taliban regime fell on 6 December 2001, and Taliban leaders fled into Pakistan and the countryside of Afghanistan.[4]

What do you think?

Was President Bush right to use force to remove the Taliban? What did the United States and the United Kingdom gain by working with the Afghans?

"Unlawful combatants"

President Bush declared that members of al-Qaeda were "unlawful combatants", rather than prisoners of war. This meant that any al-Qaeda members who were captured would not have the usual protection of international law. In addition, the prisoners could be held indefinitely without formal charges.

What do you think?

Is it ethical to hold suspects indefinitely without any formal charges being brought against them? The inmates had no legal means to defend themselves. Is this ethical?

A detainee in the controversial Camp X-Ray in Guantánamo Bay, Cuba, is taken for questioning wearing manacles.

The captured suspects were held in a US military site at Guantánamo Bay, in Cuba. This camp has caused a great deal of controversy. Some people believe, based on leaked secret files, that some inmates have been held on the flimsiest grounds and have been tortured and abused.[5] International human rights organizations have repeatedly condemned the camp, yet it has remained open. On 22 January 2009, President Barack Obama signed an order saying it should be closed but that process did not happen immediately.[6]

None of the coalition governments stopped the Guantánamo Bay site. Tony Blair said in 2005 that Guantánamo Bay was an "anomaly [rare situation]" that would have to be "dealt with" and that he would prefer if it were closed.[7] Some of the inmates were either British or used to live in the United Kingdom. In 2010, the UK government agreed to pay compensation to about a dozen men who accused UK security forces of being involved in their transfer to the Guantánamo Bay camp.[8]

TONY BLAIR

Born: 6 May 1953, Edinburgh

In 1997, Tony Blair became the youngest prime minister since 1812. He was leader of the Labour Party and took over from the Conservative government, ending its 18-year rule. Blair was influential in negotiating significant peace deals in Northern Ireland. Blair was aware of the power of promoting people, and he controversially gave important powers to unelected advisers, such as the media consultant Alistair Campbell. His early years in the spotlight are often associated with the marketing image of "Cool Britannia", which became a popular idea to promote the United Kingdom as a dynamic and successful country. Blair courted celebrities and invited pop stars to his home, in the hope of attracting a younger following to Labour. He resigned from his position of prime minister on 27 June 2007.[9]

The Iraq problem

At the same time, an undeclared conflict was continuing between the United States and United Kingdom on one side, and Iraq on the other.

Saddam Hussein ruled Iraq. His Ba'ath Party had seized control of the Iraq government in a bloodless coup (a takeover that threatens violence, but does not use it) in 1968. Saddam was deputy chairman. In 1972, Saddam nationalized the Iraqi oil industry, meaning the government took control of it. The money raised allowed Iraq to invest in social programmes and infrastructure (things like buildings and roads) and raise the standard of living in Iraq. The money also allowed him to build up the Iraqi military. In 1979, Saddam became president of Iraq, and he began a rule of terror. He used his secret police force to suppress political opponents.

The cost of battle

Iraq's relationship with its neighbour, Iran, was tense during the 1970s. In 1980, Iraq launched a full-scale invasion of Iran's oil fields, starting an eight-year war. Saddam used chemical weapons against Iranian troops and other rebels, and the UN condemned him as a result.

By the late 1980s, Saddam's Iraq owed enormous amounts of money to foreign countries. Saddam needed more money. In August 1990, he invaded Kuwait, a country with big oil reserves.[10] Saddam's plan was probably to take control of Kuwait in order to make money from its oil.

The UN authorized a military intervention, led by US troops, to free Kuwait. This was known as the Persian Gulf War (1990–1991). Afterwards, as part of the UN ceasefire agreement, Iraq was not allowed to possess biological, chemical, or nuclear weapons. But Saddam refused to allow the UN weapon inspectors into Iraq to check whether or not he had weapons.

Patience runs out

By 2001, Bush and Blair were beginning to get impatient over Saddam's lack of cooperation. They were also worried that he was hiding **weapons of mass destruction**. They gave a warning that Saddam should complete disarmament (getting rid of his weapons) or risk military action. They asked him to leave or face removal. Saddam refused.

On 20 March 2003, the United States and United Kingdom invaded Iraq alongside troops from Australia and Poland. President Bush stated that the reason for the attack was "to disarm Iraq of weapons of mass destruction, to end Saddam Hussein's support for terrorism, and to free the Iraqi people".[11]

The troops toppled Saddam from power, but he was not caught until 13 December 2003. He was tried by the Iraqi High Tribunal and found guilty of crimes against humanity, including willful killing, illegal imprisonment, and torture. He was hanged on 30 December 2006.

Saddam Hussein at his trial.

Controversy over aims

No weapons of mass destruction have been found in Iraq, and critics of Bush and Blair have accused them of misleading their countries and exaggerating the threat posed by Saddam. In 2004, the 9–11 Commission – a group in charge of investigating the September 2001 attacks – reported that there was no evidence of a relationship between Iraq and al-Qaeda.[12]

What do you think?

Do you think that Bush and Blair believed in their reasons for going to war with Iraq? Could they have had other motives? Some people think the war was about the control of Iraq's oil reserves, since the West uses so much oil.

THE STRUGGLE AGAINST CORRUPTION (1965–2008)

In a democracy, people elect politicians to act on their behalf. This places the politicians in a position of trust. However, sometimes the temptations of power become too much to resist, and politicians act inappropriately.

Corruption and abuse of power can take many forms. Examples include voter **fraud** and **extortion** (getting money through threats). Sometimes leaders will give positions of power to friends (which is called **cronyism**) or to supporters (which is called patronage). Sometimes leaders give these positions to family members, an act called **nepotism**. Sometimes leaders steal money. This has happened in both democracies and dictatorships, in all parts of the world.

Corruption

Corruption harms everyone, especially the poor. It can be found in varying degrees in every country in the world, but it is especially entrenched in Africa. For example, Nigeria, in West Africa, has large supplies of petroleum and natural gas, which means that it could be a wealthy country. But government corruption and a large national debt that needs to be repaid means that very little of Nigeria's money is actually spent on the people.[1]

In 1993, Sani Abacha seized power in Nigeria.[2] He promised a return to democracy, but instead he became a dictator, suppressed other political parties, and violated human rights. Curiously, Abacha seemed to believe in democracy, because he sent troops in to restore democracy in the countries of Liberia and Sierra Leone. He just did not want to lose power himself.[3] After his sudden death in 1998, Abacha's family returned nearly £653 million to the Nigerian government. Estimates of the amount stolen by Abacha are between £1.3 and £3.2 billion.[4]

Mobutu Sese Seko, the former president of the Central African country of Zaire (now called the Democratic Republic of the Congo), is alleged to have gained a personal fortune of about £3.3 billion. The Democratic Republic of the Congo is a country rich in natural resources such as diamonds and copper. But under Seko's rule, the country experienced neglect because of government corruption and mismanagement.[5]

General Sani Abacha, the former leader and dictator of Nigeria. He is believed to have taken the equivalent of billions of pounds from the country.

Chart of corruption

The following table shows the alleged fortunes stolen by political leaders:

Leader	Country	Date of rule	Amount in £
Suharto	Indonesia	1967–1998	£9.8–22.8 billion
Ferdinand Marcos	Philippines	1966–1986	£3.3–6.5 billion
Mobutu Sese Seko	Democratic Republic of the Congo	1965–1997	£3.3 billion
Sani Abacha	Nigeria	1993–1998	£1.3–3.3 billion
Benazir Bhutto and Asif Ali Zardari	Pakistan	1988–1990, 1993–1996, and 2008–	£979 million

Suharto

Suharto was the president of Indonesia, a country in Southeast Asia, for three decades from 1967 to 1998. During this time, he is alleged to have gained a personal fortune of £9.8 to £22.8 billion. This is one of the biggest cases of corruption among world leaders.[6]

Under Suharto's rule, Indonesia's economy grew and the standard of living for most people increased. He also introduced education and literacy (reading and writing) programmes. However, the increasing wealth of the country was not spread evenly. Suharto was accused of nepotism and cronyism, with his friends and six children becoming rich by controlling key sectors of the country's economy.

What do you think?

How can it be acceptable for a leader or government to steal from its people? How could £22.8 billion have been spent to improve the lives of the Indonesian people?

Suharto on a political visit to India in 1980. His personal gains through corruption are some of the largest ever.

By the 1990s, this corruption began to alienate people. However, because of the successful growth of the economy, Suharto remained in power. In 1997, a currency crisis affecting all of Southeast Asia showed the holes in the Indonesian economy, and the country went into recession (economic decline). Anti-government protests and riots combined with the loss of support of the military forced Suharto to resign in 1998.[7]

Cronyism, voting fraud, and shoes

In the Philippines, in Southeast Asia, Ferdinand Marcos ruled from 1966 to 1986, in a regime that was renowned for its corruption and suppression of democracy. In 1972, Marcos imposed martial law, which is when military law is used instead of normal civil rights. It is supposed to just be a temporary state in times of emergency, but Marcos kept the country under martial law for nearly 10 years.

During the time of martial law, Marcos' wife, Imelda, became a powerful political figure. She was criticized for nepotism when she gave her relatives beneficial positions in government and industry.[8] In 1986, Marcos fled the Philippines when evidence of massive voting fraud emerged. His wife left behind a collection of about 3,000 pairs of shoes. This collection came to symbolize the corruption of the Marcos regime, as millions of Filipinos were living in extreme poverty in what had become one of the poorest countries in the world.[9] It is alleged the Marcoses stole between £3.3 and £6.5 billion.[10]

In 1985, students protested against Marcos' rule by burning an effigy (model) of him.

Fighting corruption

When Benazir Bhutto (pictured below) became the prime minister of Pakistan in 1988, she became the first woman leader of a Muslim nation in modern history. She took over a country that had widespread poverty, governmental corruption, and increasing crime. By 1990, her government was dismissed from power on grounds of corruption.[11] Bhutto became the opposition against her successor, Nawaz Sharif, and in 1993, she was elected to become prime minister again. She ruled between 1993 and 1996, when allegations of corruption were renewed.[12]

Bhutto and her husband, Asif Ali Zardari, were convicted of corruption in 1999. From 1993 to 1996, Zardari had been the minister of investment and had gained the nicknames of "Mr 5 Per cent" up to "Mr 100 Per cent". He got these nicknames because it was said he demanded a percentage of government contracts issued to businesspeople. It is alleged that Bhutto and Zardari amassed more than £979 million through kickbacks, which are bribes or secret payments made in return for a favour. However, the Supreme Court overturned the conviction for corruption, because there was evidence that the government had interfered with the case.[13]

In October 2007, Bhutto was granted an official pardon, and all corruption charges were dropped.[14] Bhutto was assassinated on 27 December 2007. Her husband, Zardari, went on to become president of Pakistan in September 2008.[15] In November 2008, Bhutto was awarded the honour of a UN human rights prize for her support of democracy and human rights for women, children, and minorities.[16]

What do you think?

Should Bhutto's work for human rights and democracy be considered more important than any allegations of corruption? Does it matter if a leader is corrupt if he or she is also doing good?

President Bill Clinton embraces White House intern Monica Lewinsky at a Democratic fundraiser. The scandal surrounding their relationship stirred up many ethical questions.

Private lives

It is understandable that the public has a right to know about corruption and abuses of power when they relate to government funds and activity. But what about the details of private lives of politicians? Should they be kept private?

Bill Clinton was president of the United States from 1993 to 2001. He had some important successes in his time as president, such as achieving peace talks to end the ethnic conflict in Bosnia and Herzegovina in the 1990s, and ongoing talks to bring a resolution to the dispute between the Palestinians and Israelis. He also oversaw a large economic boom.

But a scandal clouded Clinton's presidency when it was suggested that he had an affair with a White House intern called Monica Lewinsky. Clinton publicly denied that he had an affair with Lewinsky. He was accused of encouraging Lewinsky to lie under oath and say that they had not had an affair. In 1998, Clinton faced impeachment, which means he could have been removed from office if found guilty. He was charged with perjury (lying under oath) and obstruction of justice.[17] Evidence was found that Clinton had had an affair with Lewinsky. However, in 1999, the Senate voted and determined that he would not be found guilty of perjury or obstruction of justice.[18]

LEADERS IN POLITICS

"Politics is a jungle: torn between doing the right thing and staying in office – between local interest and the national interest – between the private good of the politician and the general good."[1]

John F. Kennedy

The above quote from John F. Kennedy sums up the difficulties a leader faces while in office. Kennedy knew that doing the right thing would not always be easy. For example, Kennedy knew that his new Civil Rights Act would not be popular with many white voters (see pages 36 and 37). But when he saw the television images of the violence used against African-American protestors, some of whom were just children, Kennedy could not avoid taking action. He knew morally that he could not ignore the situation. He never found out whether this would affect his chances of re-election, however, because on 22 November 1963, he was assassinated.

German civilians were shown the bodies of the Holocaust victims so that people believed the stories and did not think it was just propaganda. People wanted to ensure that the Holocaust wouldn't ever be forgotten.

Never forgetting history

The lessons from World War II and the Holocaust taught people that we cannot turn a blind eye on suffering and persecution in any country. World leaders must act to stop it. The government had ignored Winston Churchill's warnings over the threat that Adolf Hitler's Germany posed (see pages 10 and 11). Would history have been different if, in 1938, the United Kingdom, France, and Italy had stopped Germany from taking over an area of Czechoslovakia? The memory of the horrors of World War I was still fresh in the minds of the leaders, so they were trying to avoid another war. But by avoiding the conflict, they let Hitler become more powerful.

When war was declared, the government realized it was wrong to have ignored Churchill's warning, and so he was made prime minister. Churchill became a pivotal player in the relationship between the United States and the Soviet Union. Even though he and President Franklin D. Roosevelt both had concerns over the communist beliefs of Stalin, he persuaded Roosevelt to join forces for the sake of winning the war. Churchill and Roosevelt must have considered the negatives in making this alliance with a potential enemy, but they judged that Hitler posed the more immediate risk. In joining forces, they were able to achieve the greatest good for the greatest number of people.

Sir Winston Churchill is thought of as a great statesman who played a crucial role in the Allied victory in World War II.

The threat of nuclear war

By the end of World War II, the world had discovered the power of nuclear weapons. The threat of nuclear war changed politics. Both superpowers, the United States and the Soviet Union, had nuclear weapons, so their leaders had to tread carefully – or risk triggering a nuclear war accidentally. Diplomatic relationships were more important than ever, but the superpowers found other ways to prove their dominance. They supported other countries' causes. But is it ethical to support another country's war to get at an enemy?

And what happens when the events do not quite go according to plan, as with Nikita Khrushchev and the Cuban Missile Crisis (see pages 22 and 23)? Khrushchev thought he could outwit Kennedy, but he did not expect Castro to make his own plans to start attacking US planes. Khrushchev had to find a way to back down without appearing to do so. Kennedy had to provide him with the opportunity to do so without appearing weak.

Mikhail Gorbachev perhaps did not realize that the reforms he was introducing would result in the end of communism in the Soviet Union and its eventual collapse (see pages 24 and 25). Would he have introduced these reforms if he had realized this?

How to treat your enemies

A leader must make a moral decision after capturing an enemy. There are rules set by the UN on how a prisoner of war should be treated. A leader might feel disgust and hate at what the enemy has done. But morally he or she knows that the enemy Is still u person and should be treated as such.

Is it ever justifiable to treat a person inhumanely, even if you believe that person has acted inhumanely and caused the death and suffering of thousands? Gandhi and King thought not. They believed that the use of violence was not the solution, but rather that peaceful protest would achieve better results.

The temptations of power

Sometimes the temptations of power are just too much to resist. But can a leader ever justify spending government funds on living a life of luxury when the people he or she is supposed to represent are living in poverty? There are numerous examples of leaders who have done just that.

Private lives, public business?

What rights does a leader have to a private life? Does the way a leader acts in his or her private life affect the way he or she runs the country? Does the public have the right to know if a leader is having an affair? Is the leader taking advantage of his or her position of power? What if the leader lies about it? How does this reflect upon the leader?

The ethics of politics

The world of politics is a complicated one. There are many different leaders who may all have a different set of beliefs that leads them to make different ethical decisions. It is easier to judge the past actions of a leader when we can see the whole picture of an event. It is much harder for the leader at the time to know how actions will interact with those of others to shape history.

Mobutu Sese Seko, the former president of Zaire (now the Democratic Republic of the Congo) is alleged to have gained a personal fortune at the expense of his people.

TOPICS FOR DISCUSSION

You can be the judge of whether today's leaders are behaving in an ethical manner. Choose a current situation to explore and build a case for each side. The following are some suggestions of ongoing international conflicts to examine, but there might also be more local ones that will provide some interesting debate.

Afghanistan

How are political leaders handling the situation in Afghanistan? There has been a change in leadership since the invasion in 2001. What difference has this made? How quickly should troops pull out of Afghanistan? What will happen if they do? Are the Afghan government and army strong enough to remain in power? Will the Taliban regain control of the country? If you need to, read pages 38 and 39 to remind yourself of why US and UK troops are in Afghanistan. You could also research the history of Afghanistan and find out about the Soviet invasion of Afghanistan in 1979.

Pakistan

The situation in Pakistan is currently unstable. The territory of Kashmir is still disputed between Pakistan and India. Both countries have nuclear weapons, so a conflict between them could have worldwide repercussions.

After the September 2001 attacks in the United States, Pakistan stopped supporting the Taliban regime in Afghanistan and became an ally of the United States. However, the discovery of al-Qaeda leader Osama bin Laden in Pakistan in 2011 has caused tensions to grow between Pakistan and the United States.

Investigate how US president Barack Obama handled the raid that resulted in the death of Osama bin Laden. Obama ordered that bin Laden be given an Islamic burial in accordance with his religion, and for the body to be buried at sea. Obama has refused to release photos showing bin Laden after he was killed. Do you think Obama acted ethically in these decisions?

Iraq

Since the removal of Saddam Hussein in 2003, Iraq has been a volatile country. All US troops were supposed to leave Iraq by the end of 2011, but a top Iraqi army officer warned that the Iraqi military might not be ready to take control. What will the United States do?

Iran

With Russian help, Iran has built its first nuclear power station, but it says its nuclear ambitions are peaceful. However, the UN is concerned, and so it imposed sanctions on Iran in 2010. Investigate the latest situation and how the leaders are negotiating with each other.

North Korea

North Korea is one of the most secretive countries in the world. It is still under communist rule after the death of Kim Jong-il in December 2011. His youngest son, Kim Jong-un, has taken over the leadership. The state is accused of human rights abuses. There are also worldwide concerns about North Korea's nuclear ambitions. Diplomatic efforts have been intense, in an effort to make North Korea agree to shut down its main nuclear reactor in return for aid. However, conflicts with South Korea in 2010 set back relations. Find out what the world's leaders are doing to try to put an end to this threat to world peace.

GLOSSARY

agrarian relating to the cultivation of land

alliance agreement to cooperate

ally country cooperating with another for a specific purpose

apartheid policy of racial segregation in South Africa

assassinate kill a political or religious leader

boycott refuse to use a service or to buy goods

capitalism economic and political system in which trade and industry are controlled by private companies for profit

Central Intelligence Agency (CIA) part of US government concerned with foreign intelligence and counterintelligence

chancellor head of government in Germany

civil disobedience way of protesting by refusing to obey certain laws or pay taxes

civil rights rights of an individual to freedom and equality

coalition temporary alliance of people or countries to do a joint action

Cold War period of tension and military threats between the US and the Soviet Union, each supported by their allies. The Cold War lasted from the end of World War II to about 1991.

communism political theory that states that all property should be publicly owned

communist person who believes in communism

concentration camp prison camps set up by the Nazis to detain or kill political prisoners, Jews, gypsies, homosexuals, and the disabled

congress group of people called together for a special purpose; when capitalized, it refers to the lawmaking body of the United States

corrupt fraudulent

corruption use of corrupt practices such as bribery or fraud

cronyism favouring friends by giving them jobs

cult of personality means by which a sense of devotion is created among a leader's followers

democracy political system in which the leaders are voted for by the citizens of a country

democratic relating to a democracy

dictator ruler with total power. Often the ruler has come to power by force.

dictatorship state ruled by a dictator

diplomatic international relations

economic way a country's economy is controlled

economy wealth and resources of a country or region, especially in terms of goods and services that it buys or produces

ethical morally correct

ethics study of human morals

exile person who has been banished from his or her own country

extortion getting money through threats

fraud criminal deception

Holocaust mass murder of Jews and others by the German Nazi regime in concentration camps during World War II. About 6 million Jews were killed in the Holocaust.

media television, newspapers, and radio

militant aggressive political activist

monarchy form of government in which leadership is hereditary, meaning it is passed down within a family

nepotism favouring family members by giving them jobs

neutral not taking either side of a dispute

non-alignment policy of not taking sides and trying to remain neutral

nuclear weapons weapons that use nuclear energy

persecute victimize

political relating to the government

political system way that a government is run

politics way a government runs the country and its relations with other countries

regime particular government

sanction restriction imposed on a country – such as restricting what it can sell or buy – in order to force it to change its policies

segregation separation of different races of people

sit-in occupy a place as a form of protest

Soviet Union country made up of what are now Russia, Ukraine, and several other countries. The Soviet Union opposed the United States and its allies in the Cold War. The country broke up in 1991.

superpower country that has a dominant position in world politics

Taliban extreme Islamic group that believes that women should be virtually excluded from public life. The group has enforced harsh punishment for crimes, including chopping off hands for even the most minor crime, and public executions. It came to power in Afghanistan in the 1990s.

United Nations (UN) international organization set up after World War II to promote international peace

weapons of mass destruction chemical, biological, or nuclear weapons that can cause widespread death and destruction

NOTES ON SOURCES

Politics and ethics (pp. 4–7)

1. *Encyclopædia Britannica*, "Political economy", http://library.eb.co.uk/eb/article-9060632.

2. http://www.jfklibrary.org/JFK/Life-of-John-F-Kennedy.aspx?p=4

3. *Britannica Student Encyclopedia*, "Adolf Hitler", http://library.eb.co.uk/all/comptons/article-202062.

4. *Encyclopædia Britannica*. "Martin Luther King, Jr.", http://library.eb.co.uk/eb/article-3917.

5. African Success, "Biography of Nelson Mandela", http://www.africansuccess.org/visuFiche.php?id=373&lang=en

Leaders during war: World War II (pp. 8–15)

1. *Britannica Junior Encyclopedia*, "World War II", http://library.eb.co.uk/all/elementary/article?articleId=442095.

2. David Taylor, *Leading Lives: Adolf Hitler* (Oxford: Heinemann Library, 2001), 14.

3. Ibid., 15.

4. Ibid., 14.

5. Ibid., 27.

6. *Encyclopædia Britannica*, "Hitler youth", http://library.eb.co.uk/eb/article-9040609.

7. David Cesarani, "From Persecution to Genocide", BBC History, http://www.bbc.co.uk/history/worldwars/genocide/radicalisation_01.shtml.

8. Taylor, *Hitler*, 30.

9. *Britannica Student Encyclopedia*, "Winston Churchill", http://library.eb.co.uk/all/comptons/article-198624.

10. Simon Seabag Montefiore, *Speeches That Changed the World* (London: Quercis Publishing, 2010), 9314; *Encyclopædia Britannica*, "Munich Agreement", http://library.eb.co.uk/eb/article-9054283.

11. Montefiore, *Speeches That Changed the World*, 93–94.

12. Ibid., 95

13. *Encyclopædia Britannica*, "Franklin D. Roosevelt", http://library.eb.co.uk/eb/article-23949.

14. Geoffrey Best, "Winston Churchill: Defender of Democracy", BBC History, http://www.bbc.co.uk/history/worldwars/wwtwo/churchill_defender_01.shtml#four.

15. *Encyclopædia Britannica*, "Winston Churchill", http://library.eb.co.uk/eb/article-60596.

16. *Britannica Student Encyclopedia*, "Winston Churchill".

17. Ibid.

18. *Britannica Student Encyclopedia*, "Joseph Stalin", http://library.eb.co.uk/all/comptons/article-208604.

19. *Encyclopædia Britannica*, "Union of Soviet Socialist Republics", http://library.eb.co.uk/eb/article-42058.

20. *Encyclopædia Britannica*, "German-Soviet Nonaggression Pact", http://library.eb.co.uk/eb/article-9036574.

21. *Encyclopædia Britannica*, "Joseph Stalin", http://library.eb.co.uk/eb/article-13392.

22. *Encyclopædia Britannica*, "German-Soviet Nonaggression Pact".

The Cold War (1945–1991) (pp. 16–25)

1. *Britannica Student Encyclopedia*, "Cold War", http://library.eb.co.uk/all/comptons/article-9273726.

2. Peter Chrisp, *20th Century Leaders: Kennedy* (London: Wayland, 2002), 22.

3. Chrisp, *Kennedy*, 23.

4. *Britannica Student Encyclopedia*, "Fidel Castro", http://library.eb.co.uk/all/comptons/article-9273554.

5. Chrisp, *Kennedy*, 24–25.

6. *Encyclopædia Britannica*, "John F. Kennedy", http://library.eb.co.uk/eb/article-3868.

7. Chrisp, *Kennedy*, 27.

8. Ibid., 28.

9. *Encyclopædia Britannica*, "Fidel Castro", http://library.eb.co.uk/eb/article-9020736.

10. *Britannica Student Encyclopedia*, "John F. Kennedy", http://library.eb.co.uk/all/comptons/article-203382.

11. *Encyclopædia Britannica*, "John F. Kennedy".

12. *Encyclopædia Britannica*, "Ronald W. Reagan", http://library.eb.co.uk/eb/article-214232.

13. *Encyclopædia Britannica*, "Margaret Thatcher", http://library.eb.co.uk/eb/article-214939.

14. *Encyclopædia Britannica*, "Strategic Defense Initiative", http://library.eb.co.uk/eb/article-9069901.

15. Archie Brown, "Reform, Coup and Collapse: The End of the Soviet State", BBC History, http://www.bbc.co.uk/history/worldwars/coldwar/soviet_end_01.shtml.

The fight for civil rights (1915–1994) (pp. 26–37)

1. *Britannica Student Encyclopedia*, "Mahatma Gandhi", http://library.eb.co.uk/comptons/article-9274487.

2. Montefiore, *Speeches That Changed the World*, 65.

3. *Encyclopædia Britannica*, "Mohandas Karamchand Gandhi", http://library.eb.co.uk/eb/article-22634.

4. *Encyclopædia Britannica*, "Mohandas Karamchand Gandhi".

5. *Encyclopædia Britannica*, "Jawaharlal Nehru", http://library.eb.co.uk/eb/article-5157.

6. *Encyclopædia Britannica*, "Mohandas Karamchand Gandhi".

7. *Encyclopædia Britannica*, "Jawaharlal Nehru".

8. Ibid.

9. *Encyclopædia Britannica*, "Nelson Mandela", http://library.eb.co.uk/eb/article-282994.

10. Nelson Mandela, *Long Walk to Freedom* (London: Abacus, 1995), 130.

11. Ibid., 182.

12. Ibid., 182–83.

13. *Britannica Student Encyclopedia*, "Apartheid", http://library.eb.co.uk/all/comptons/article-9272908.

14. *Encyclopædia Britannica*, "Nelson Mandela".

15. Montefiore, *Speeches That Changed the World*, 149–50.

16. Mandela, *Long Walk to Freedom*, 503.

17. *Britannica Student Encyclopedia*, "Apartheid".

18. *Encyclopædia Britannica*, "Nelson Mandela".

19. African Success, "Biography of Nelson Mandela", http://www.africansuccess.org/visuFiche.php?id=373&lang=en.

20. David Downing, *Leading Lives: Martin Luther King* (Oxford: Heinemann Library, 2002), 11.

21. *Encyclopædia Britannica*, "Martin Luther King, Jr", http://library.eb.co.uk/eb/article-3916.

22. Ibid.

23. Ibid.

24. Downing, *Martin Luther King*, 32.

25. Ibid., 34.

26. Downing, *Martin Luther King*, 37.

27. Montefiore, *Speeches That Changed the World*, 145.

The global war on terror (2001–2011) (pp. 38–43)

1. *Encyclopædia Britannica*, "September 11 attacks", http://library.eb.co.uk/eb/article-9394915.

2. Montefiore, *Speeches That Changed the World*, 209.

3. *Encyclopædia Britannica*, "September 11 attacks".

4. *Encyclopædia Britannica*, "Afghanistan War", http://library.eb.co.uk/eb/article-292841.

5. David Leigh, James Ball, Ian Cobain, and Jason Burke, "Guantánamo Leaks Lift Lid on World's Most Controversial Prison", *The Guardian*, 25 April 2011, http://www.guardian.co.uk/world/2011/apr/25/guantanamo-files-lift-lid-prison.

6. *Encyclopædia Britannica*, "Guantánamo Bay detention camp", http://library.eb.co.uk/eb/article-9473907.

7. *The Guardian*, "Blair: Guantánamo Is an Anomaly", 17 February 2006, http://www.guardian.co.uk/uk/2006/feb/17/politics.guantanamo.

8. BBC News, "Government to Compensate ex-Guantánamo Bay Detainees," 16 November 2010, http://www.bbc.co.uk/news/uk-11762636.

9. *Encyclopædia Britannica*, "Tony Blair", http://library.eb.co.uk/eb/article-277074.

10. *Britannica Student Encyclopedia*, "Saddam Hussein", http://library.eb.co.uk/all/comptons/article-9274996.

11. White House Archives, "President Discusses Beginning of Operation Iraqi Freedom", 22 March 2003, http://georgewbushwhitehouse.archives.gov/news/releases/2003/03/20030322.html.

12. *Encyclopædia Britannica*, "George W. Bush", http://library.eb.co.uk/eb/article-278444.

The struggle against corruption (1965–2008) (pp. 44–49)

1. *Encyclopædia Britannica*, "Nigeria", http://library.eb.co.uk/eb/article-9110793.

2. *Britannica Book of the Year: 1998*, "Sani Abacha", http://library.eb.co.uk/eb/article-9114504.

3. *Encyclopædia Britannica*, "Sani Abacha", http://library.eb.co.uk/eb/article-9389478.

4. International Centre for Asset Recovery, "Sani Abacha", http://www.assetrecovery.org/kc/node/52f770df-a33e-11dc-bf1b-335d0754ba85.0;jsessionid=01B7A8151D999055BC1790CF5D342AF9.

5. BBC News, "Suharto Tops Corruption Rankings", 25 March 2004, http://news.bbc.co.uk/1/hi/3567745.stm.

6. Ibid. 7. *Encyclopædia Britannica*, "Suharto", http://library.eb.co.uk/eb/article-9070191.

7. *Encyclopædia Britannica*, "Suharto," http://library.eb.co.uk/eb/article-9070191.

8. *Encyclopædia Britannica*, "Ferdinand E. Marcos", http://library.eb.co.uk/eb/article-9050814.

9. *BBC News*, "Homage to Imelda's Shoes", 16 February 2001, http://news.bbc.co.uk/1/hi/world/asia-pacific/1173911.stm.

10. International Centre for Asset Recovery, "Ferdinand Marcos", http://www.assetrecovery.org/kc/node/5881e61f-a33e-11dc-bf1b-335d0754ba85.4%20.4.

11. *Encyclopædia Britannica*, "Benazir Bhutto", http://library.eb.co.uk/eb/article-9079076.

12. International Centre for Asset Recovery, "Benazir Bhutto", http://www.assetrecovery.org/kc/node/8ef5b614-4391-11de-9627-1d322f879051.3.

13. *Encyclopædia Britannica*, "Benazir Bhutto".

14. International Centre for Asset Recovery, "Benazir Bhutto".

15. BBC News, "Profile: Asif Ali Zardari", 16 December 2009, http://news.bbc.co.uk/1/hi/world/south_asia/4032997.stm.

16. UN News Centre, "Benazir Bhutto Named Among Seven Winners of UN Human Rights Prize", 26 November 2008, http://www.un.org/apps/news/story.asp?NewsID=29090&Cr=human+rights&Cr1=prize.

17. *Encyclopædia Britannica*, "Bill Clinton", http://library.eb.co.uk/eb/article-215395.

18. *Encyclopædia Britannica*, "Impeachment of a president", http://library.eb.co.uk/eb/article-9476624.

Leaders in politics (pp. 50–53)

1. Chrisp, *Kennedy*, 15.

FIND OUT MORE

Books

Benazir Bhutto: Pakistani Prime Minister and Activist (Signature Lives),
   Mary Englar (Compass Point Books, 2006)
Martin Luther King (Famous People), Anna Clayborne (Wayland, 2008)
Nelson Mandela (Famous People), Hakim Adi (Wayland, 2008)
Who's in Charge? (Dorling Kindersley, 2010)
Winston Churchill (Famous Lives), Katie Daynes (Usborne, 2006)

DVDs

World War II: Behind Closed Doors (2009): This series tells of Stalin's
meetings with the Nazis, Churchill, and Roosevelt.
Gandhi (1982): This Oscar-winning film tells the story of Gandhi's life.
Cry Freedom (1987): This drama is about the South African black activist
Steve Biko.

Websites

www.number10.gov.uk/history-and-tour/past-prime-ministers/
Use the timeline on this website to discover more about prime ministers
mentioned in this book.

www.winstonchurchill.org
This website is full of information about Winston Churchill.

www.apartheidmuseum.org/resources
Discover more about apartheid in South Africa.

www.assetrecovery.org/kc/node/1698185c-4768-11dd-a453-b75b81bfd63e.html
Investigate more cases of corruption.

memory.loc.gov/ammem/aaohtml/exhibit/aointro.html
Learn more about African Americans' struggle for civil rights.

www.mkgandhi.org
This website features lots of information about Gandhi.

INDEX